White Pine

Other Books by Mary Oliver

White Pine

POEMS AND PROSE POEMS

Mary Oliver

Harcourt Brace & Company

New York   San Diego   London

Requests for permission to make copies of any part of the work should be mailed
to: Permissions Department, Harcourt Brace & Company, 6277 Sea Harbor Drive,
Orlando, Florida 32887-6777.

"Morning Glories" and "Fall" copyright © 1994 by *Poetry*.

Library of Congress Cataloging-in-Publication Data
Oliver, Mary, 1935–
White pine: poems and prose poems/Mary Oliver.—1st ed.
p.   cm.
ISBN 0-15-100131-6
ISBN 0-15-600120-9 (Harvest: pbk.)
I. Title.
PS3565.L5W45   1994
811'.54—dc20   94-20112

Designed by Lydia D'moch

Printed in the United States of America
First edition
A B C D E

Publication acknowledgments appear on
page 57, which constitutes a continuation
of the copyright page.

For
Molly Malone Cook

Contents

White Pine

Work

How beautiful
this morning
was Pasture Pond.

It had lain in the dark, all night,
catching the rain

on its broad back.
All day I work
with the linen of words

and the pins of punctuation
all day I hang out
over a desk

grinding my teeth
staring.
Then I sleep.

Then I come out of the house,
even before the sun is up,

and walk back through the pinewoods
to Pasture Pond.

Hummingbirds

The female, and the two chicks,
each no bigger than my thumb,
scattered,
shimmering

in their pale-green dresses;
then they rose, tiny fireworks,
into the leaves
and hovered;

then they sat down,
each one with dainty, charcoal feet—
each one on a slender branch—
and looked at me.

I had meant no harm,
I had simply
climbed the tree
for something to do

on a summer day,
not knowing they were there,
ready to burst the ledges
of their mossy nest

and to fly, for the first time,
in their sea-green helmets,
with brisk, metallic tails—
each tulled wing,

with every dollop of flight,
drawing a perfect wheel
across the air.
Then, with a series of jerks,

they paused in front of me
and, dark-eyed, stared—
as though I were a flower—
and then,

like three tosses of silvery water,
they were gone.
Alone,
in the crown of the tree,

I went to China,
I went to Prague;
I died, and was born in the spring;
I found you, and loved you, again.

Later the darkness fell
and the solid moon
like a white pond rose.
But I wasn't in any hurry.

Likely I visited all
the shimmering, heart-stabbing
questions without answers
before I climbed down.

You stand inside the lime-green house of the salt marsh and you hear a faint, gritty music. It does not rise then fall like the wind rounding a distant corner; it does not explode suddenly, like the heron you rustled up from the glossy storerooms of water. It simply remains, dull and constant. It is everywhere.

And then you see them. Snails.

Snails gliding on the sticky thumbs of their bodies up and down the stems and blades of the marsh grass, and across the damp sand, everywhere, sucking and scraping whatever it is they eat—algae, things too small to have a name that you know. Above the hurried murmur of the draining water, the snails, flowing and eating, are making the sound you hear. You do not find

the tufts of their bodies attractive. When you look at them, nothing happens, not like the startle of your heart when the heron rises, or when the wind shutters shut then opens and falls over the hill. Still, you know this

moment is important, like a page from an ancient document, found in a dusty jar, in a dry cave. Who are we? What are our chances? Where have we made the terrible mistake we must turn from, or perish? The snails

are everywhere, nibbling, sucking, climbing the billows of sand, shuffling up into the marshes, by the millions, all doing something incredible. Not pretty, but incredible. You lift

your own delicate hands, you touch your lips.

What lay on the road was no mere handful of snake. It was the copperhead at last, golden under the street lamp. I hope to see everything in this world before I die. I knelt on the road and stared. Its head was wedge-shaped and fell back to the unexpected slimness of a neck. The body itself was thick, tense, electric. Clearly this wasn't black snake looking down from the limbs of a tree, or green snake, or the garter, whizzing over the rocks. Where these had, oh, such shyness, this one had none. When I moved a little, it turned and clamped its eyes on mine; then it jerked toward me. I jumped back and watched as it flowed on across the road and down into the dark. My heart was pounding. I stood a while, listening to the small sounds of the woods and looking at the stars. After excitement we are so restful. When the thumb of fear lifts, we are so alive.

At dawn
   the big dog—
      Winston by name—
         reached down

into the leaves—tulips and willows mostly—
   beside the white
      waterfall,
         and dragged out,

into plain sight,
   a fawn;
      it was scarcely larger
         than a rabbit

and, thankfully,
   it was dead.
      Winston
         looked over the

delicate, spotted body and then
   deftly
      tackled
         the beautiful flower-like head,

breaking it and
   breaking it off and
      swallowing it.
         All the while this was happening

it was growing lighter.
    When I called to him
        Winston merely looked up.
            Grizzled around the chin

and with kind eyes,
    he, too, if you're willing,
        had a face
            like a flower; and then the red sun,

which had been rising all the while anyway,
    broke
        clear of the trees and dropped its wild, clawed light
        over everything.

How necessary it is to have opinions! I think the spotted trout lilies are satisfied, standing a few inches above the earth. I think serenity is not something you just find in the world, like a plum tree, holding up its white petals.

The violets, along the river, are opening their blue faces, like small dark lanterns.

The green mosses, being so many, are as good as brawny.

How important it is to walk along, not in haste but slowly, looking at everything and calling out

Yes! No! The

swan, for all his pomp, his robes of glass and petals, wants only to be allowed to live on the nameless pond. The catbrier is without fault. The water thrushes, down among the sloppy rocks, are going crazy with happiness. Imagination is better than a sharp instrument. To pay attention, this is our endless and proper work.

Three women
climb from the car
in which they have driven slowly
into the churchyard.
They come toward us, to see
what we are doing.
What we are doing
is reading the strange,
wonderful names
of the dead.
One of the women
speaks to us—
after we speak to her.
She walks with us and shows us,
with a downward-thrust finger,
which of the dead
were her people.
She tells us
about two brothers, and an argument,
and a gun—she points
to one of the slabs
on which there is a name,
some scripture, a handful of red
plastic flowers. We ask her
about the other brother.
"Chain gang," she says,
as you or I might say
"Des Moines," or "New Haven." And then,
"Look around all you want."
The younger woman stands back, in the stiff weeds,

like a banked fire.
The third one—
the oldest human being we have ever seen in our lives—
suddenly drops to the dirt
and begins to cry. Clearly
she is blind, and clearly
she can't rise, but they lift her, like a child,
and lead her away, across the graves, as though,
as old as anything could ever be, she was, finally,
perfectly finished, perfectly heartbroken, perfectly wild.

Where
the porcupine is
I don't
know but I hope

it's high
up on some pine
bough in some
thick tree, maybe

on the other side
of the swamp.
The dogs have come
running back, one of them

with a single quill
in his moist nose.
He's laughing,
not knowing what he has

almost done
to himself.
For years I have wanted to see
that slow rambler,

that thornbush.
I think, what love does to us
is a Gordian knot,
it's that complicated.

I hug the dogs
and their good luck,
and put on their leashes.
So dazzling she must be—

a plump, dark lady
wearing a gown of nails—
white teeth tearing skin
from the thick tree.

A single swallow glides in the air above the water. Next to it something hovers, thin and white. It flies too—or is it floating? It vanishes. It appears again, a little smaller than the bird.

Now the bird approaches land. Now it is over the beach itself. The floating object is also over the beach. A feather!

The swallow snaps the feather from the air and holds it in its beak while it takes three or four rapid strokes forward. Then it lets the feather go, and dives away.

The feather pauses on the updraft, then begins to descend. The bird turns, flows back, glides above and beneath it. The feather tumbles erratically. With a plunge the swallow snaps it from the air and flies on, and then, again, lets it go.

All of this is repeated maybe a dozen times. Finally the swallow ignores the feather, which drifts toward the berms of wild roses, between the dunes and the sea. The swallow climbs higher into the air, blue shoulders pumping hard. Then it swings, glides, turns toward the sea, is gone.

This morning
    two deer
        in the pinewoods,
            in the five A.M. mist,

in a silky agitation,
    went leaping
        down into the shadows
            of the bog

and together
    across the bog
        and up the hill
            and into the dense trees—

but once,
    years ago,
        in some kind of rapturous mistake,
            the deer did not run away

but walked toward me
    and touched my hands—
        and I have been, ever since,
            separated from my old, comfortable life

of experience and deduction—
    I have been, ever since,
        exalted—
            and even now,

though I miss the world
    I would not go back—
        I would not be anywhere else
            but stalled in the happiness

of the miracle—
    every morning
        I stroll out into the fields,
            I believe in everything—

I believe in anything—
    even if the deer are wild again
        I am still standing under the dark trees,
            they are still walking toward me.

here I go
into the wide gardens of
wastefields blue glass clear glass
and other rubbishes blinking from the

dust from the fox tracks among the
roots and risings of
buttercups joe pye honey

suckle the queen's
lace and her

blue sailors

the little wrens
have carried a hundred sticks into

an old rusted pail and now they are
singing in the curtains of leaves they are

fluttering down to the bog they are dipping

their darling heads down to wet

their whistles how happy they are to be
diligent at last

foolish birds

Mockingbirds

This morning
two mockingbirds
in the green field
were spinning and tossing

the white ribbons
of their songs
into the air.
I had nothing

better to do
than listen.
I mean this
seriously.

In Greece,
a long time ago,
an old couple
opened their door

to two strangers
who were,
it soon appeared,
not men at all,

but gods.
It is my favorite story—
how the old couple
had almost nothing to give

but their willingness
to be attentive—
and for this alone
the gods loved them

and blessed them.
When the gods rose
out of their mortal bodies,
like a million particles of water

from a fountain,
the light
swept into all the corners
of the cottage,

and the old couple,
shaken with understanding,
bowed down—
but still they asked for nothing

beyond the difficult life
which they had already.
And the gods smiled as they vanished,
clapping their great wings.

Wherever it was
I was supposed to be
this morning—
whatever it was I said

I would be doing—
I was standing
at the edge of the field—
I was hurrying

through my own soul,
opening its dark doors—
I was leaning out;
I was listening.

Those who disappointed, betrayed, scarified! Those who would still put their hands upon me! Those who belong to the past!

How many of us have weighted the years with groaning and weeping? How many years have I done it how many nights spent panting hating grieving, oh, merciless, pitiless remembrances!

I walk over the green hillsides, I lie down on the harsh, sun-flavored blades and bundles of grass; the grass cares nothing about me, it doesn't want anything from me, it rises to its own purpose, and sweetly, following the single holy dictum: to be itself, to let the sky be the sky, to let a young girl be a young girl freely—to let a middle-aged woman be, comfortably, a middle-aged woman.

Those bloody sharps and flats—those endless calamities of the personal past. Bah! I disown them from the rest of my life, in which I mean to rest.

At the Lake

A fish leaps
like a black pin—
then—when the starlight
strikes its side—

like a silver pin.
In an instant
the fish's spine
alters the fierce line of rising

and it curls a little—
the head, like scalloped tin,
plunges back,
and it's gone.

This is, I think,
what holiness is:
the natural world,
where every moment is full

of the passion to keep moving.
Inside every mind
there's a hermit's cave
full of light,

full of snow,
full of concentration.
I've knelt there,
and so have you,

hanging on
to what you love,
to what is lovely.
The lake's

shining sheets
don't make a ripple now,
and the stars
are going off to their blue sleep,

but the words are in place—
and the fish leaps, and leaps again
from the black plush of the poem,
that breathless space.

Blue Heron

Like a pin
of blue lightning
it thrusts
among the pads,

plucking up
frogs, flipping them
in mid-air, so that they
slide, neatly

face-first, down
the long throat.
I don't know
about God,

but didn't Jesus say:
"This is my body,"
meaning, the bread—
and meaning, also,

the things of this world?
This isn't really
a question.
It is the hard

and terrible truth
we live with,
feeding ourselves
every day.

The bird
stared again into the water,
and dashed forward a little,
and stabbed

and swallowed,
and then just stood there
shining,
like a blue rose.

Blue and dark-blue
   rose and deepest rose
      white and pink they

are everywhere in the diligent
   cornfield rising and swaying
      in their reliable

finery in the little
   fling of their bodies their
      gear and tackle

all caught up in the cornstalks.
   The reaper's story is the story
      of endless work of

work careful and heavy but the
   reaper cannot
      separate them out there they

are in the story of his life
   bright random useless
      year after year

taken with the serious tons
   weeds without value humorous
      beautiful weeds.

Our neighbor, tall and blonde and vigorous, the mother of many children, is sick. We did not know she was sick, but she has come to the fence, walking like a woman who is balancing a sword inside of her body, and besides that her long hair is gone, it is short and, suddenly, gray. I don't recognize her. It even occurs to me that it might be her mother. But it's her own laughter-edged voice, we have heard it for years over the hedges.

All summer the children, grown now and some of them with children of their own, come to visit. They swim, they go for long walks along the harbor, they make dinners for twelve, for fifteen, for twenty. In the early morning two daughters come to the garden and slowly go through the precise and silent gestures of T'ai Chi.

They all smile. Their father smiles too, and builds castles on the shore with the children, and drives back to the city, and drives back to the country. A carpenter is hired—a roof repaired, a porch rebuilt. Everything that can be fixed.

June, July, August. Every day, we hear their laughter. I think of the painting by van Gogh, the man in the chair. Everything wrong, and nowhere to go. His hands over his eyes.

The last dollar went, then the last dime. Then I went out to the dunes behind the harbor, where the roses cover the berms and also grow thickly and randomly on the slopes of pale sand, and are lively with bees, and a deep honey-smell, and I lay down.

I could see the ocean. Far out it was shaking with light, and boats with their white sails full of the invisible wind moved back and forth. All along the shore the water rolled and rolled its bales of silver.

After a while I got up, as from the dead—it was that wonderful to be, at last, entirely poor, and happy.

I found some weeds I could eat. I found some wild washed boards, could they not make a simple house?

Some laughing gulls flew by, with their perfect black faces, their coral-colored legs.

In a sudden crease of hills there was a green place, like a salad. At its center a little freshwater pond, from which I drank.

The sun shone.

*

Oh Jesus, poor boy, when was it you saw, clearly and irrevocably, just where you were headed?

Opossum

The dogs descend,
prancing and loping, ready to brawl, but it
lies down, as always, and plays
dead,

and so I have
a good look, in the starlight,
at the monkey tail, and the stumped lightning of the teeth,
and the spidery hands,

and the eyes which
won't focus, won't
look at me. It is
a small pig with a savage head—

a bloated flute, lying
in the wet grass.
I call the dogs away
and I think very soon they forget—

but all day I imagine
how it got up, slowly, when we were gone,
and sighed, and shook itself—
how it minced away

down the old ditches—how it scurried
through the damp leaves, to some pleated
circlet of slumped oak.
All day the dogs

are gone on their rounds of adventures—
and as for myself—at any cost
it is the present I lay claim to—
it is the dangerous and marvelous future

I mean to find.
And yet, how it stays in my mind—
a little landslide of perfect responses—
a gray baby ghost,

its pale snout turning,
its five-fingered spider hands tapping,
in drowsy circles,
the mossy banks of the past.

Owl in the Black Oaks

If a lynx, that plush fellow,
climbed down a
tree and left behind
his face, his thick neck,

and, most of all, the lamps of his eyes,
there you would have it—
the owl,
the very owl

who haunts these trees,
choosing from the swash of branches
the slight perches and ledges
of his acrobatics.

Almost every day
I spy him out
among the knots and the burls,
looking down

at his huge feet,
at the path curving through the trees,
at whatever is coming up the hill
toward him,

and, though I'm never ready—
though something unspeakably cold
always drops through my heart—
it is a moment

as lavish as it is fearful—
there is such pomp
in the gown of feathers
and the lit silk of the eyes—

surely he is one of the mighty kings
of this world.
Sometimes, as I keep coming,
he simply flies away—

and sometimes the whole body
tilts forward, and the beak opens,
clean and wonderful,
like a cup of gold.

I walk through a grove of pines and startle the nighthawk from the limb where it has been lying, resting or sleeping. The bird is similar in color to the gray limb, and lies *along* not across it, so is almost invisible. On its hawk-like wings it rises into the sky, and vanishes.

The nighthawk doesn't nest here but only stops a few days on its long travels. I know this one must be tired of flight, and I am sorry to have disturbed it.

The next day, walking the same woods, I approach with care. The bird is again resting on the limb, its eyes shut. I back away and do not disturb it.

The following year, almost to the day, I enter the pinewoods and remember the nighthawk just in time—in time to be cautious and silent. And the bird is there, in the same tree, on the same limb, in the pinewoods that is so pretty and so restful, apparently, to both of us.

1. Woodshed

For weeks
the center of the universe
is the woodshed
which I keep filling,

which I keep
emptying and filling,
working
every morning

in the light-soaked yard
among the heaps of pink oak,
yellow birch,
red pine.

Sometimes I rest a little.
Then I gaze out from the yard
into the world, or I gaze
into myself.

But mostly I give attention
to what I'm doing—
cutting, chopping, stacking.
I have a good time.

This is how it is,
year after year—
everything put by,
nothing kept,

everything used up.
And that, as much as anything,
is the wonder of it,
I say philosophically—

how it all
gathers and vanishes,
how it all
goes up in smoke.

2.

But there's this, too:
the little words
leaping up like hairs!

3. *Teeth*

Out of my desire to be
related to my sleek young dog, I ate
her puppy teeth, all of them I could find, white and
crisp, each one rolled in a
pad of bread. I was not, consequently,
related to her. But I say this:
in any life some failures are nevertheless
achievements, and this one, in mine, is by no means
the least. God help us if
we make this world only out of bone, and not the greater weight
of admiration, whimsy,
                    fierce and unspeakable love.

4.

Goodbye, goodbye,
to the black oaks.

This morning the mockingbird
halfway up the pale dune, and only
a pitchpine for pulpit, offered

with infrangible exactitude:

phoebe,
robin, blue jay, flicker,
towhee, goldfinch, ovenbird, titmouse,
linnets, grackle, bobwhite, cardinal,
carolina wren, chickadee, nuthatch, english
sparrow, crested flycatcher, then he

flung his body into the air.

6.

May I also bring to each blue and cloudy morning a
suitable exuberance, a few exact

words, bowing and snapping.

7. *Submitting to Tests*

It is late summer, and the pond is not what it was. The sun has
drawn away most of the water, so that here and there nothing
remains but the spongy green base. It is a little Dismal. It ticks
and pulses faintly. Somewhere the frogs, in the last wet inches,
leap, or they do not leap, I merely hear their silvery whinnies.
There is a green heron with a yellow eye. I remember him, in the

shimmering wheel of spring; with red legs he flew past, busy with
his life. But, as everywhere, the changes have come. The heron is
tired. The pond, rusty and slick, is tired. Frayed, full of nets and
shadows. Still vital, still interesting. But tired.

I lie down on the high cold table, and they begin.

8. *The Garden*

What I want to know, please, is
what is possible, and what is not.
If it is not, then I am for it.
My heart is out of its flesh-phase.
I am done with all of it, the habits, the patience.
Whoever I was, it is growing hazy and forgettable.

Whoever I am, it is for mere appearance's sake.
It is for coin, and foolishness,
and I am thinking of something better.
All morning it has been raining.
In the language of the garden, this is happiness.
The tissues perk and shine.
Truly this is the poem worth keeping.
A mossy house anyone with any sense would enter
as soon as the soul begins
to desire the impossible.

I have never felt so young.

9.

Still, listen, I swear, I have not set one word down
on top of another without
breathing into it!

On the hottest day of summer
I thought of a place
on a knoll
and under some pines
where a breeze might come
flowing out of the bog

so I went there

but a beautiful woman
who had thought of it first
was lying casually
just where I'd thought to lie down
don't move I said
but she rose up
on her pretty hooves
at the sound of my voice
and heavily
and with sorrow and with panic
she vanished
into the trees.

11.

Each moment has been so slow and so full
and so drenched in sweetness and my life
has gone by so fast

12. The Swans

Once in Ohio
of all places

I saw
hundreds of swans
they came
out of the sky
like an orchard
getting married
to the dark lake
no one knew
they were coming
we heard them we looked up we began shouting
they skidded down
into the water
which broke and swirled
in excitement
embracing their white breasts
their black feet
in the morning
we returned early they were waking
they were rising up
their wings creaking and whistling
then they flew away
my life in Ohio
went on
everything was changed
do you know what I'm saying
everything
everything was changed

13.

Goodbye goodbye
to the blue iris

This is not song, this is not singing, this is not thoughtful, it comes from no idea, it is only heat and good cheer, or, even less, nervousness, the grim melodious anxiety of the beast, the announcement that something more than inertia is present and recognizes the fact of evening, a click in the brain; or sees, and nothing to do about it, black snake twining up trunk and branches toward nest, and still the bead of the heart must make

a noise about it, its one noise, a waterfall of noise—no thought, no idea, simply noise, call it noise, which rises through the leaves, not out of them but through them; all creatures are

beneath us, ah, yes, in the order of things.

But, listen. Listen.

Each voice shimmers; yet it is one voice: the damp and sonorous exaltation of the dead, or the not-yet-born, who still know everything.

On the dog's ear, a scrap of filmy stuff
    turns out to be
a walking stick, that jade insect, this one scarcely sprung
    from the pod of the nest,
not an inch long. I could just see
the eyes, elbows, feet nimble under the long shanks.
    I could not imagine it could live
in the brisk world, or where it would live, or how. But
    I took it
outside and held it up to the red oak that rises
    ninety feet into the air, and it lifted its forward-most
        pair of arms
with what in anything worth thinking about would have seemed
    a graceful and glad gesture; it caught
onto the bark, it hung on; it rested; it began to climb.

I found a dead fox
beside the gravel road,
curled inside the big
iron wheel

of an old tractor
that has been standing,
for years,
in the vines at the edge

of the road.
I don't know
what happened to it—
when it came there

or why it lay down
for good, settling
its narrow chin
on the rusted rim

of the iron wheel
to look out
over the fields,
and that way died—

but I know
this: its posture—
of looking,
to the last possible moment,

back into the world—
made me want
to sing something
joyous and tender

about foxes.
But what happened is this—
when I began,
when I crawled in

through the honeysuckle
and lay down,
curling my long spine
inside that cold wheel,

and touched the dead fox,
and looked out
into the wide fields,
the fox

vanished.
There was only myself
and the world,
and it was I

who was leaving.
And what could I sing
then?
Oh, beautiful world!

I just lay there
and looked at it.
And then it grew dark.
That day was done with.

And then the stars stepped forth
and held up their appointed fires—
those hot, hard
watchmen of the night.

Toad

I was walking by. He was sitting there.

It was full morning, so the heat was heavy on his sand-colored head and his webbed feet. I squatted beside him, at the edge of the path. He didn't move.

I began to talk. I talked about summer, and about time. The pleasures of eating, the terrors of the night. About this cup we call a life. About happiness. And how good it feels, the heat of the sun between the shoulder blades.

He looked neither up nor down, which didn't necessarily mean he was either afraid or asleep. I felt his energy, stored under his tongue perhaps, and behind his bulging eyes.

I talked about how the world seems to me, five feet tall, the blue sky all around my head. I said, I wondered how it seemed to him, down there, intimate with the dust.

He might have been Buddha—did not move, blink, or frown, not a tear fell from those gold-rimmed eyes as the refined anguish of language passed over him.

There is a tree here so beautiful it even has a name. Every morning, when it is still dark, I stand under its branches. They flow from the thick and silent trunk. One can't begin to imagine their weight. Year after year they reach, they send out smaller and smaller branches, and bunches of flat green leaves, to touch the light.

Of course this has consequences. Every year the oak tree fills with fruit. Just now, since it is September, the acorns are starting to fall.

I don't know if I will ever write another poem. I don't know if I am going to live for a long time yet, or even for a while.

But I am going to spend my life wisely. I'm going to be happy, and frivolous, and useful. Every morning, in the dark, I gather a few acorns and imagine, inside of them, the pale oak trees. In the spring, when I go away, I'll take them with me, to my own country, which is a land of sun and restless ocean and moist woods. And I'll dig down, I'll hide each acorn in a cool place in the black earth.

To rise like a slow and beautiful poem. To live a long time.

Neighbors described

the high, rough-coated shoulders

the long neck

the glandular bell hanging

the shy face

the modest face of a scholar

weary of reading
in the dim light

of the forest, how he carried

the flared rack

the knobs the branches

of dense horn

sign of power

and how he walked

shaking the flies

rippling his dark pelt

ponderous on his long bones

into the water

and how he lifted

frond after frond

lilies and rushes

onto the path

of his grinding molars

the light lingered

we sat on the shore

and talked in whispers

watched the herons

heard the owl

greeted the moon

stared at the far shore
stared at the far shore

empty in the moonlight

What lay this morning
on the wet sand
was so ugly
I sighed with a kind of horror as I lifted it

into my hand
and looked under the soaked mat of what was almost fur,
but wasn't, and found
the face that has no eyes, and recognized

the sea mouse—
toothless, legless, earless too,
it had been flung out of the stormy sea
and dropped

into the world's outer weather, and clearly it was
done for. I studied
what was not even a fist
of gray corduroy;

I looked in vain
for elbows and wrists;
I counted
the thirty segments, with which

it had rippled its mouse-like dance
over the sea's black floor—not on
feet, which it did not have, but on
tiny buds tipped with bristles,

like paintbrushes—
to find and swallow
the least pulse, and so stay alive, and feel—
however a worm feels it—satisfaction.

Before me
the sea still heaved, and the heavens were dark,
the storm unfinished,
and whatever was still alive

stirred in the awful cup of its power,
though it breathe like fire, though it love
the lung of its own life.
Little mat, little blot, little crawler,

it lay in my hand
all delicate and revolting.
With the tip of my finger
I stroked it,

tenderly, little darling, little dancer,
little pilgrim,
gray pouch slowly
filling with death.

Now there's William. He comes pecking, like a bird, at my heart. His eyebrows are like the feathers of a wren. His ears are little seashells.

I would keep him always in my mind's eye.

Soon enough he'll be tall, walking and conversing; he'll have ideas, and a capricious will; the passions will unfold in him, like greased wheels, and he will leap forward upon them.

Who knows, maybe he'll be an athlete, quick and luminous; or a musician, bent like a long-legged pin over the piano's open wing; or maybe he will stand day after day over a draftsman's desk, making something exquisite and useful—a tower or a bridge.

Whatever he does, he'll want the world to do it in. Maybe, who knows, he'll want this very room which, only for convenience, I realize, I've been calling mine.

I feel myself begin to wilt, like an old flower, weak in the stem.

But he is irresistible! Whatever he wants of mine—my room, my ideas, my glass of milk, my socks and shirts, my place in line, my portion, my world—he may have it.

Fall

the black oaks
fling their bronze fruit
into all the pockets of the earth
    pock pock

they knock against the thresholds
the roof the sidewalk
fill the eaves
    the bottom line

of the old gold song
of the almost finished year
what is spring all that tender
    green stuff

compared to this
falling of tiny oak trees
out of the oak trees
    then the clouds

gathering thick along the west
then advancing
then closing over
    breaking open

the silence
then the rain
dashing its silver seeds
    against the house

Near Wolfeboro,
near the vast, sparkling lake,
deep in the woods,
I swing

my legs over
the old wall and sit
on the iron-cold
stones. The wall

is longer
than any living thing, and quieter
than anything
that breathes, as we

understand breathing. It turns,
it cuts back, it approaches again.
It knows
all the angles.

Somebody
raised it
stone by stone, each lagging weight
pulling the shoulders.

Somebody
meant to sheet these green hills
with domesticity,
and did, for a while.

But not anymore.
And now the unmaking
has, naturally, begun.
Stones fall—

tilt and fall—
but slowly—
only a few a year—
into the leaves, or roll

down into the creeks, or into
the sappy knees
of the pines.
The birds

sing their endless
small alphabets.
Sometimes
a porcupine

hauls itself up and over—
or a deer
makes light of all of it,
leaping and leaping.

But mostly
nothing seems to be happening—
borders and divisions,
old sheep-holders,

the stones just sit there,
mute and tight, and wait
for the instant, gray and wild.
This morning

something slips,
and I see it all—the yearning,
then the blunt and paunchy flight,
then the sweet, dark falling.

Spiders

In fall, in the garden and the fields beyond, in the delicate yellow space between anything, spiders, plump as acorns, spin their webs; they are the wildest woven things; they are the most shimmering death-traps.

The mouse and the vole, the raccoon and fox walk lightly through the grass below. They scarcely glance up to see her running on her dark and cunning legs along the first bridges, or racing back and forth along the silver girders, or waiting, or wrapping the white moth whose night was full of bad luck, who already can't move, and will soon be dead.

What is the spider good for? A few things surely. Birds eat spiders, thus feeding the song. And spiders eat insects, some of which, as we know, carry diseases—though not *pride*—not that one.

But, speaking of that. At dawn, the early walker, to the spider a giant, wanders through the garden and the fields in the meditative, and thus inattentive, frame of mind of first things. This is, of course, myself. And more than once I have just noticed the dew-glittering web in time, and the spider stamping her tiny feet and screeching: I live here, duck your head.

Wind and rain
                then it grows colder
ice gathers
                on the barbed wire
bounding the empty field
                then six deer
walk from under the dark pines
                their heads high
their eyes soft and alert
                their legs fragile-seeming
though they are not fragile
                inside the house
it is warm and cozy
                in the *Iliad*, which I have been reading,
Achilles has just refused
                to put on his beautiful armor
yet he has said that his friend Patroclus
                might wear it
and now he is watching his darling
                as he straps the elaborate and heavy armor
over his gleaming body
                just as though there was a way
to do something in this world
                and be by the gods unnoticed
Patroclus will not come back
                from the long day's fighting
rash and sorry
                prideful and angry
Achilles will swirl and swirl, like the wind
                it comes to nothing
but a brave story
                you would think the deer

would go back to the thick pines
            but still they stand in the field
gazing and gazing
            see how their beautiful bodies
darken and tremble
            see the white rain
come down
            over their eyes.

Because it is winter
and everything in the world
is hungry,
it doesn't take long

for this hundredweight of death
to vanish. The ribs fall open
under the clouds of snow—
and the staring, antlered

head is hauled off—
even the neighborhood dogs—
my own among them—
pluck and tear and go running

under the trees—oh, it's not pretty
how they ransack
the parts of that body—
the ribs and the hooves

and the rungs of the spine—
until they are scattered
over the hills and along
the clattering creek—

until they are all carried away
in the teeth of the weasels
and the cheeks of the woodrats—
until it is done

as it must be done—
perfectly,
without levity or argument—
as though it were a dance—

the only one
that could outwit winter—
as though the life of everything
were in it.

do you know
  the old stories
    about the stars the
      hunter and dog swan crab
       dragon lion big bear and
        little bear the seven
          sisters there on the horizon call it

pleasure call it
  comfort call it
    rinsing out the dread all
      night long the silence of the
       heavens remains
         intractable the darkness is more dark
        than the back

of the moon's silver
  eye and heavy
    as lead this is why
      there are so many stories to draw
       each star into the mouth for a single
        minute to feel that white fire
         against the teeth bearable even

intimate what happens
  next we say what happens
    next and why does it
      happen and what happens
       then because *that* has happened
        lifting up the darkness
         by that much.

Then the deer stepped from the woods. It walked from the shadows under the trees into a clear space. Antlers sprang from its brow, each with five or six tines. From the antlers, from each tine, green leaves were growing, as if from the branches of a tree.

The deer stood without moving, brutish and graceful as deer alive in the daylight, except that its heavy, elaborate head was carrying, upon the usual curvatures of horn, these branches, this fountain of leaves.

Then it turned and vanished. In shyness, perhaps. Or simply because we get no more than such dreamy chances to look upon the real world. The great door opens a crack, a hint of the truth is given—so bright it is almost a death, a joy we can't bear—and then it is gone.

My dog came through the pinewoods dragging a dead fox—ribs and a spine, and a tail with the fur still on it. Where did you find this? I said to her, and she showed me. And there was the skull, there were the leg bones and the shoulder blades.

I took them home. I scrubbed them and put them on a shelf to look at—the pelvis, and the snowy helmet. Sometimes, in the pines, in the starlight, an owl hunches in the dense needles, and coughs up his pellet—the vole or the mouse recently eaten. The pellets fall through the branches, through the hair of the grass. Dark flowers of fur, with a salt of bones and teeth, melting away.

In Washington, inside the building of glass and stone, and down the long aisles, and deep inside the drawers, are the bones of women and children, the bones of old warriors. Whole skeletons and parts of skeletons. They can't move. They can't even shiver. Mute, *catalogued*—they lie in the wide drawers.

So it didn't take long. I could see how it was, and where I was headed. I took what was left of the fox back to the pinewoods and buried it. I don't even remember where. I do remember, though, how I felt. If I had wings I would have opened them. I would have risen from the ground.

There isn't anything in this world but mad love. Not in this world. No tame love, calm love, mild love, no so-so love. And, of course, no reasonable love. Also there are a hundred paths through the world that are easier than loving. But, who wants easier? We dream of love, we moon about, thinking of Romeo and Juliet, or Tristan, or the lost queen rushing away over the Irish sea, all doom and splendor. Today, on the beach, an old man was sitting in the sun. I called out to him, and he turned. His face was like an empty pot. I remember his tall, pale wife; she died long ago. I remember his daughter-in-law. When she died, hard, and too young, he wept in the streets. He picked up pieces of wood, and stones, and anything else that was there, and threw them at the sea. Oh, how he loved his wife. Oh, how he loved young Barbara. I stood in front of him, not expecting any answer yet not wanting to pass without some greeting. But his face had gone back to whatever he was dreaming. Something touched me, lightly, like a knife-blade. I felt I was bleeding, though just a little, a hint. Inside I flared hot, then cold. I thought of you. Whom I love, madly.

I Looked Up

I looked up and there it was
among the green branches of the pitchpines—

thick bird,
a ruffle of fire trailing over the shoulders and down the back—

color of copper, iron, bronze—
lighting up the dark branches of the pine.

What misery to be afraid of death.
What wretchedness, to believe only in what can be proven.

When I made a little sound
it looked at me, then it looked past me.

Then it rose, the wings enormous and opulent,
and, as I said, wreathed in fire.

The sun rises late in this southern county. And, since the first thing I do when I wake up is go out into the world, I walk here along a dark road. There are many trees. Also, shrubs and vines—sumac, the ivies, honeysuckle. I walk between two green and leafy walls.

Occasionally a rabbit leaps across the road, or a band of deer, tossing their heads and bounding great distances. Maybe some of them leap from the earth altogether. Couldn't there be pastures beside the lakes of the stars? Isn't everything, in the dark, too wonderful to be exact, and circumscribed?

For instance, the white pine that stands by the lake. Tall and dense, it's a whistling crest on windy mornings. Otherwise, it's silent. It looks over the lake and it looks up the road. I don't mean it has eyes. It has long bunches of needles, five to each bundle. From its crown springs a fragrance, the air is sharp with it. Everything is in it. But no single part can be separated from another.

I have read that, in Africa, when the body of an antelope, which all its life ate only leaves and grass and drank nothing but wild water, is first opened, the fragrance is almost too sweet, too delicate, too beautiful to be borne. It is a moment which hunters must pass through carefully, with concentrated and even religious attention, if they are to reach the other side, and go on with their individual lives.

And now I have finished my walk. And I am just standing, quietly, in the darkness, under the tree.

Publication Acknowledgments

Grateful acknowledgment is made to the periodicals in which the following poems and prose poems first appeared, sometimes in slightly different form:

The American Voice: Spiders
Amicus: Wings
Appalachia: The Gesture; Snails; Fletcher Oak
The Atlantic Monthly: The Sea Mouse; Mockingbirds
Columbia: Work; Owl in the Black Oaks
Harvard Magazine: Early Morning, New Hampshire; I Found a Dead Fox
The New York Times: I Looked Up
The Ohio Review: Grass; Roses; September
Poetry: Hummingbirds; August; Beside the Waterfall; Fall; Morning Glories
Southern Review: In Pobiddy, Georgia
Virginia Quarterly Review: The Pinewoods

JUL 0 5 1996 AUG 1996	DATE DUE	

c.1

50